ARANZI

MACHINE GUN

vol. **2**

H·a·p·p·i·n·e·s·s

U·n·h·a·p·p·i·n·e·s·s

Pigtail Girl

Square Boy

Dinosaur

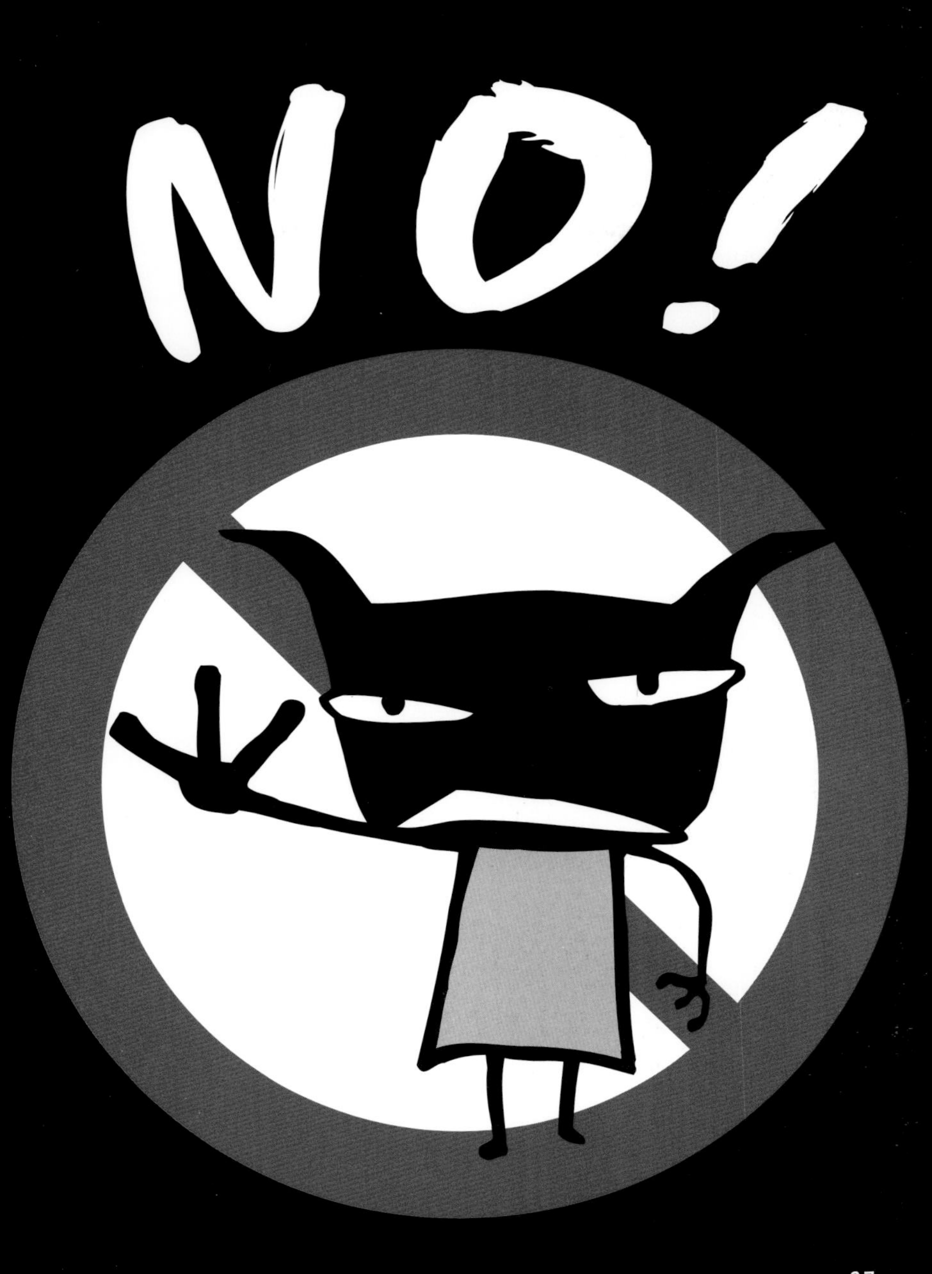
NO!

I don't feel like
doing anything.
It's all so boring.

Everyone looks happy,
even Liar.
I'm jealous.

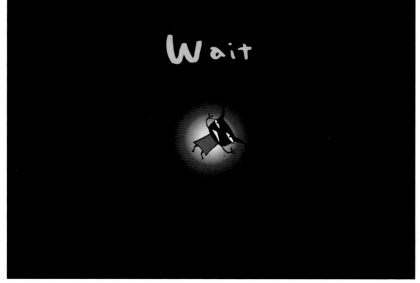

Who am I?
His Royal Badness, the Bad Guy!
Overflowing with
super badness power
from the depths of my being!

Zippity doo dah,
Zippity ay!
My, oh my .....
NO
TRESPASSING

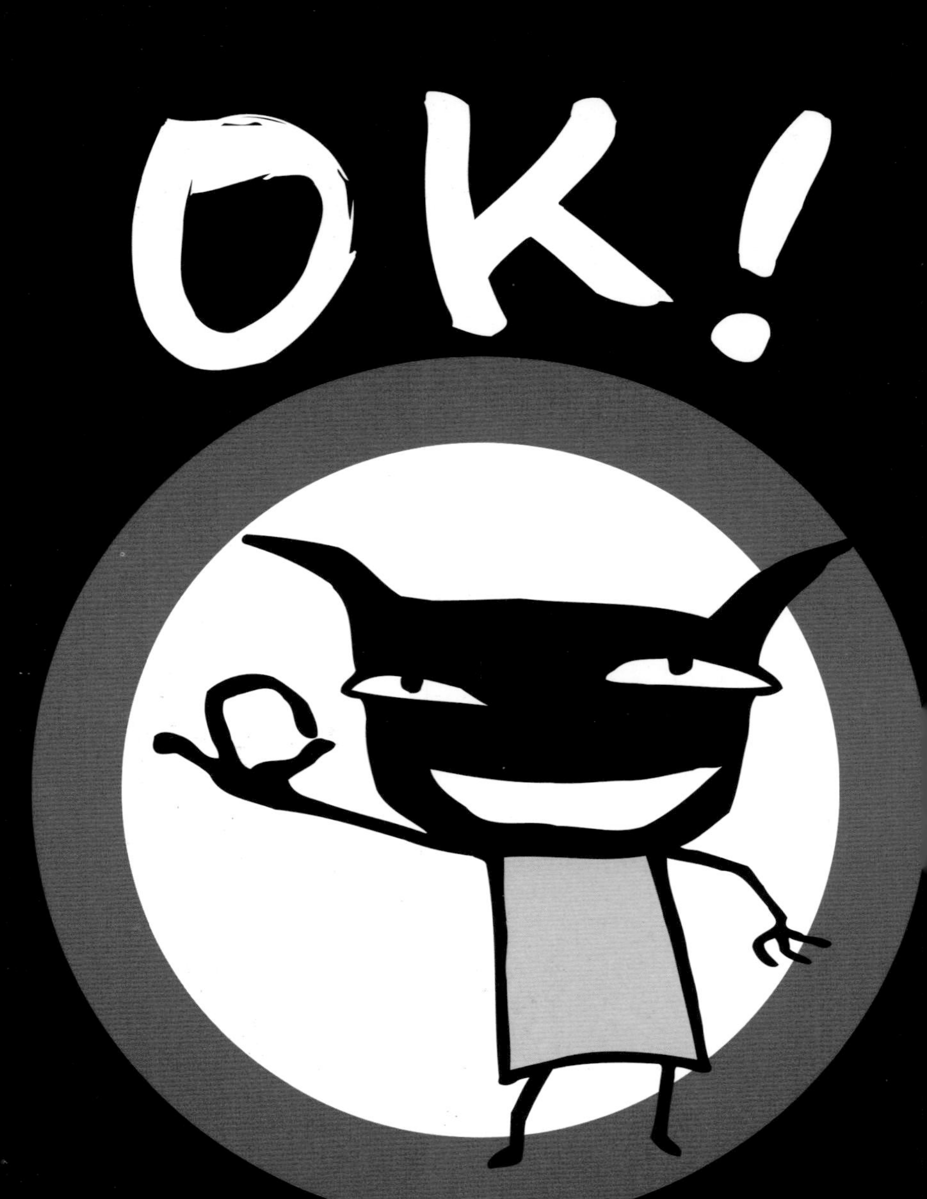
OK!

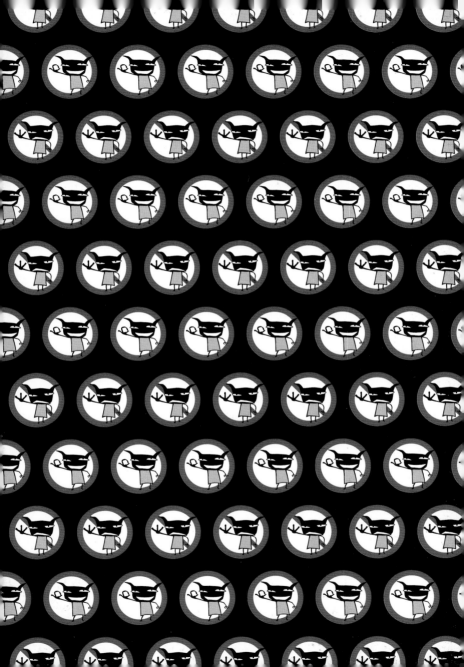

Rabbity Rabbit and Silky Kay

You know what, Silky Kay? Your hair's a mess.

What the?

How dare you, Rabbity!

Ow, Kay, that hurts!

Realizing that girls would die without cute stuff,
White Rabbit and Brown Bunny decided to find some.

23

Aaaaaaah!!! This place is packed with cute stuff!

I can't believe they were able to find all this cute stuff. I guess that's what makes them cute stuff professionals.

Ah! This is cute, too! And this... and this... How do they find these things?

Please teach us the secrets of finding cute stuff!

Wander around all the flea markets. Sometimes cute things are hidden under piles of other stuff, but the cute things naturally catch your eye. I go all the time, so my cuteness antenna works really well.

 Where do you go to find these things?

 Lately I've been going to Russia and other countries in Northern and Eastern Europe. They have a lot of things that are simple and cute.

 There's some slightly scary stuff here too. Why is that?

 Even more than things that are just cute, I like objects that tell you something about who used them or where they came from—objects that tell a story.

 Do you get sad when you go out of your way to find cute stuff, only to have someone buy it from you so it's not yours anymore?

 I'm just happy to see cute things in the hands of people who like them. If buying such objects sucks them into the world of cute stuff, all the better!

 Miss Store Manager, how would you define cute?

 Let's see... For me, cute things are the things you just can't help collecting and always having around you. It's just natural!

Bird-shaped Candle Holder

I chose this because I like birds. The hand-painted patterns on the wings are cute.

Danish Picture Book

There are a lot of stories where birds appear. The pictures are cute, and the small size is also cute!

Miss Store Manager shows us her favorite cute things and explains what makes them cute.

Freddie Cookie Cutter

I actually made cookies out of this pattern and they were really cute! You'll feel really close to Freddie.

French Grocery Store Blackboard

They stick these in boxes of vegetables to tell you the price. This came from a box of cucumbers.

Russian Alphabet Flashcards

They tell you how to pronounce them on the back. I think foreign alphabets are cute... and I love the feel of the plastic.

Russian Deck of Cards

It's cute how the balance of the diamond and club marks is different from ours. I also like the checker pattern on the backs, which gives them a real retro feel.

I really learned a lot.

Yeah, I feel like the Way of Cute Stuff has come into view a little.

"Whenever I get cute stuff, more cute things start to appear, and then I want them too.
There's no end to the search for cute stuff..."

Mulling over Miss Store Manager's words,

White Rabbit and Brown Bunny become more and more obsessed with their cute stuff expedition...

Sprite Kong had a cavity.

Spritekin was worried about him.

Teeth with cavities should be pulled out!

But Spritekin wasn't strong enough.

It wouldn't come out!

That's when another Sprite Kong with a cavity showed up.

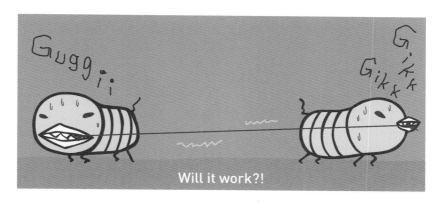

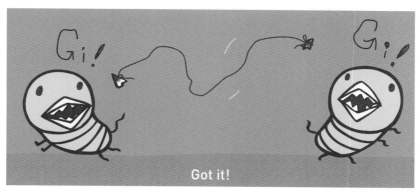

Stylish Lizard

The Lizard family is a big one with many kids.
One day, one of the kid lizards said to the mother lizard,
"Mom, I'm tired of being naked! People can't tell who's who!
I want to express myself through fashion!"
"Such a strange child," the gentle mother lizard thought,
but went ahead and made some clothes for him.

"Yay!"
Clothed, the kid lizard was happy.
Now, he wanted to try on different styles.

● Casual ●

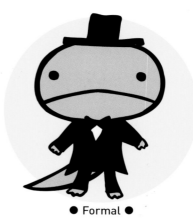

● Formal ●

So the kid lizard gave different styles a try
and realized that dressing up is a lot of fun.
(But sometimes, feeling unstylish
whatever the outfit thanks to his big head,
the kid lizard felt sad and wished for a smaller head.)

● Old man ●

● Aranzi smock ●

These days, this is his style of choice.

Name: Terry (Teh-ree)

Answers to: Terry! Terrykins. Terr-terr.
Terry-boy. Fatso (he's gained weight)

Sex: A man among men

Date of birth: June 12, 2000

Breed: Wirehaired Fox Terrier

Occupation: Store employee, model

Favorite foods: Likes all edibles (dog food, so-so)

Pastimes: Eating, hanging around parks alone,
hot springs

Special skills: Running away, real fast. (fangs bared)
Chomping on people's hands and wriggling his head,
which hurts a lot

Personality: Selfish, snappy, clingy

Celebrity dogs
don't get
any privacy,
woof!

Hmph

Terry's Head

His memory is really poor. The first word he learned was "cookie," and since then he hasn't learned much else.

Terry's Forehead

Fluffy. It's healing to pet it, but then your hand will smell like dog.

Terry's Ears

Floppy. Sometimes they turn inside out and he looks like some strange animal. Sometimes he pretends not to hear you when you call him, even though he does.

Terry's Cheeks

Gaunt and sunken, shabby and unattractive. We hide that by making his fur there really fluffy.

Terry's Mouth

He has fearsome canines but his lower teeth are crooked, so we're thinking of taking him to the orthodontist for braces.

Terry's Eyes

Small, beady, almond-shaped eyes.

Terry's Nose

When it's black and wet, it means he's healthy. When it's black and not wet, it means he's unhealthy.

Terry's Neck

It's thick and makes him seem tough (like he's middle-aged). Even his leash is made of manly black leather.

Terry's Back

The patch of black fur along the back is what makes Fox Terriers look cool, but Terry's is sprinkled with white, like an old man's salt-and-pepper hair.

Terry's Tail

He can't hide his joy.

Terry's Butt

We trim the fur so he doesn't get dingleberries. Sometimes he farts. His farts smell a hundred times worse than the average fart.

Terry's Forelegs

He'll pretend he's a cat and lick his forelegs and wipe his face, but because it's just pretend he doesn't really get clean.

Terry's Belly

Nice and smooth with no fur. Has spots like a cow's. He seems to like it when you pet him there, because he'll start wriggling if you do.

Terry's Hind Legs

They have no endurance, so even when he's told to sit he has to sit on his haunches.

39

Mr. Sprite's
Voyage

~ It Rains in My Heart ~

I felt a sudden urge to see Mt. Fuji, so I started driving.

On the way, I spent a night at
a hot spring resort in the foothills.

Will I be face to
face with Mt. Fuji
tomorrow?

This is supposed to be the best place to catch a view of Mt. Fuji! But the clouds are dense, and Mt. Fuji won't show itself.

Oh, well. I guess I'll feed the carp.

I wait for
Mt. Fuji in
the kitchen
in my room
at the inn.

Ah...

And now
it's started to rain.

Out back, there's a pond where you're supposed to see Mt. Fuji's reflection. Dang it!

Pffft...

But I buy souvenirs anyway.

Rain

At least I can check out
the Mt. Fuji museum...

Closed? You gotta be kidding me...

I start driving and eventually I see Mt. ...

Arrgh!

Gone again...

The Nimble Goblin

Voodoo Doll

Guardian Spirit

Scary Guy

I scare people easily......

so when I meet people I try to smile and seem friendly, but that just scares them even more.

So then I try some jokes, like, umm...

"Just because I have a third eye doesn't mean I deserve the third degree .....har har har!"

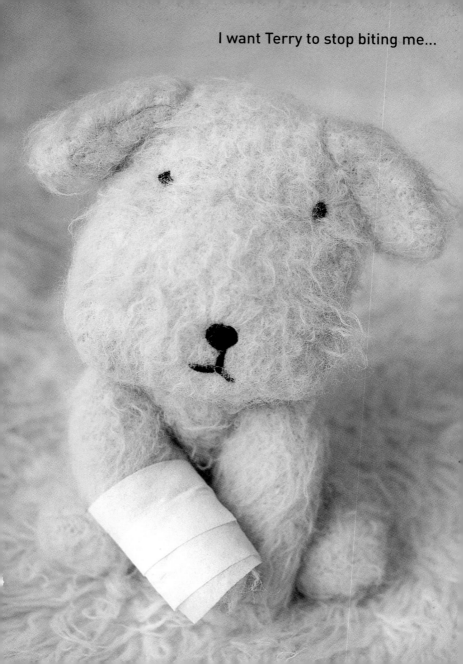

I want Terry to stop biting me...

On the Other Side

Sometimes I'm not here.

I go to other planets and make friends with people like this.

Or I go into the woods and find mushrooms that can cure any disease.

I thought everyone was like that, but...

People like that

I always think about Jambalayan (the name of a prince, it seems).

People not like that

I think about things like where I'll be going on Sunday...

Along with my turtle, I've been to outer space and to an uninhabited island (where there were man-eating tigers!). I've even spent a month in the desert.

I'm invincible!

But over here, I cry about stuff like spilling miso soup on my turtle.

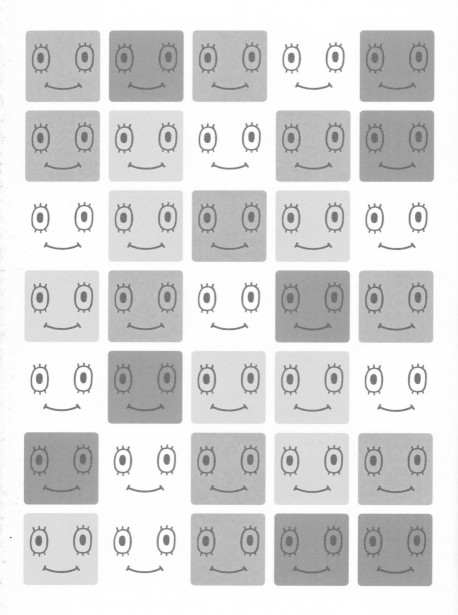

Welcome to

Mr.

Face's

Room!

Mr. Face is on the boxes.
The faces tell you
how the boxes feel.
The boxes look like
they're having fun!

Mr. Face is on the cushions.
The faces tell you
how the cushions feel.
Looks like they want to be
friends with Terry.

Mr. Face shows up on
the refrigerator too.
And the trash can!
The faces tell you
how the refrigerator
and the trash can feel.
Looks like they get along
really well.

Mr. Face is even on the toilet.
The face tells you how the toilet feels.
The toilet is going to try to bite your butt!
It's plotting some kind of mischief.
Be careful.

Capricorn

Isn't it surprising to know that
goats eat paper?
I'm not sure why, but if you put this
appliqué on your notebook covers and
book covers and stationery containers,
they turn into good luck charms.
Isn't that reassuring?

Aquarius

Putting this appliqué on objects
near water in your kitchen or
bathroom, like your toilet lid cover,
will ward off evil. Try it out.
It can't hurt.

Pisces

This appliqué makes you good
at swimming. It's best to put it
on your swimsuit. If that's the last
place you'd be willing to put it, then
just put it on your swimsuit bag.
But then it'll only work half as well.

71

hee hee hee
hee hee
hee hee hee
hee hee hee hee
hee hee hee
hee hee hee
hee hee

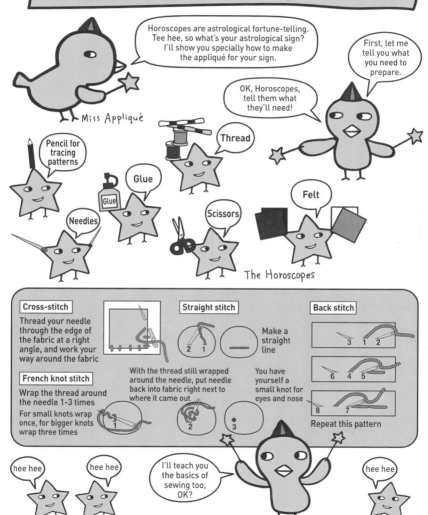

Make Your Own Astrological Sign

by Miss Appliqué

Horoscopes are astrological fortune-telling. Tee hee, so what's your astrological sign? I'll show you specially how to make the appliqué for your sign.

First, let me tell you what you need to prepare.

Miss Appliqué

OK, Horoscopes, tell them what they'll need!

Pencil for tracing patterns

Thread

Glue

Felt

Needles

Scissors

The Horoscopes

Cross-stitch
Thread your needle through the edge of the fabric at a right angle, and work your way around the fabric

French knot stitch
Wrap the thread around the needle 1-3 times
For small knots wrap once, for bigger knots wrap three times

Straight stitch
Make a straight line

With the thread still wrapped around the needle, put needle back into fabric right next to where it came out

You have yourself a small knot for eyes and nose

Back stitch

Repeat this pattern

hee hee

hee hee

I'll teach you the basics of sewing too, OK?

hee hee

73

74

This one's for you, Taurus.

Hat

White of eyes (2 pieces)

Pupils (2 pieces)

Be sure to apply your Taurus appliqué onto your leather goods.

Body

Snout

Black spots

Taurus, done.

The nostrils should be done with French knots

Hat   Hat

Body   Body

Cut in slits here

This one's for you, Gemini.

Twins!

White of eyes for the chick on left (2 pieces)

Pupils for the chick on left (2 pieces)

White of eyes for the chick on right (2 pieces)

Pupils for the chick on right (2 pieces)

Top beak (2 pieces)

Bottom beak (2 pieces)

Feet should be straight stitched

Gemini, done.

White of eyes (2 pieces)

Pupils (2 pieces)

This one's for you, Cancer.

Claw   Claw

Hat

Body

Arms and legs should be backstitched

Mouth should be straight stitched

All these appliqué patterns can be reduced/enlarged, so you can make them any size you want!

Cancer, done.

Face

Impressive mane

Body

Tip of tail

This one's for you, Leo.

Hat

White of eyes (2 pieces)

Pupils (2 pieces)

Mouth

We recommend enlarging the pattern 150%.

The tail and teeth should be straight stitched

Leo, done.

75

This one's for you, Virgo.

Hair

Face

Use a French knot for the center of the flower
Straight stitch the flower's stem

Flower

White of eyes (2 pieces)
Pupils (2 pieces)

Hat

Mouth should be straight stitched

Dress

How to make the arms and legs

1 2 3 4

Virgo, done.

Face

Beak

White of eyes (2 pieces)

Pupils (2 pieces)

Pans

Hat

Dress

This one's for you, Libra.

Stop playing on the scales, Horoscopes!

The scale beam can be done with either a straight stitch or backstitch

Libra, done.

This one's for you, Scorpio.

Claw   Claw

White of eyes (2 pieces)
Pupils (2 pieces)

Hat

Tail

Scorpio, done.

Arms and legs should be backstitched

I'll tell you the secret to happiness:

Beak

Face

White of eye
Pupil

Hat

This one's for you, Sagittarius.

Feather

The bow portion shoul be backstitched

Sagittarius, done.

Hee hee hee, you must appliqué your sign on everything around you and never stop!

Hee hee

76

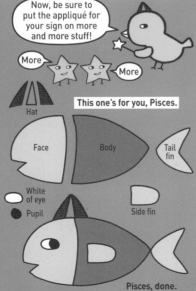

When I think of Osaka,
I think of octopus balls and
Dotonbori Street, where
you'll find many eateries.

Let's cuten things up with The Cute Book

$12.95/$16.00 CND

Full of patterns and introductions to characters.

They're easy to make and easier to love.

The Bad Book stars the one and only Bad Guy, along with his unbelievably bad friend, Liar.

$12.95/$16.00 CND

You want to see a really bad book?

No.

Argh! It's So Cute!!

ARANZI MACHINE GU
vol. 1

The Aranzi Machine Gun series
is no firearm catalog.
It's a massive assault of
cuteness and ridiculousness,
with a special craft section
at the end of every issue,
to make practical use of
the hilarious (if useless)
inside scoops you got in
the rest of the book.

$9.95/$12.95 CND